CONTENTS

KU-131-933

mo22158

WHAT IS ADOLESCENCE?

Adolescence is the time when children change physically and emotionally into young adults. It's a bridge between childhood and adulthood. It's a time of uncertainty, a time that can be exciting and frustrating, happy and scary, interesting and boring. It's unpredictable, and it's different from any other time in your life.

Doctors describe adolescence as the time between puberty (when most young people become fertile) and the point at which they stop growing. Adolescents describe it as the time when they start wanting to do their own thing and nobody will let them. Parents think of it as the time when their children get stroppy and disobedient.

Left Adolescence is known as being a time of emotional and physical turmoil. Yet for many teenagers it is a time of discovery and excitement.

Right Adolescence is when teenagers start to develop their personality and discover who they are.

WHEN DOES ADOLESCENCE START?

There are no set ages for adolescence. It can start as young as nine or as late as 17. It can last as little as two years, or five years or more. The start and finish can be affected by your genes, your diet and your lifestyle.

THE MALE AND FEMALE BODY

PREPARING FOR ADOLESCENCE

Adolescence doesn't have to be miserable. It can even be fun! The more people know about the physical and emotional changes which occur in adolescence, and what causes them, the more ready they are to deal with them. If you know what to expect, you can prepare for things like periods, wet dreams, spots and moods. You can also get ready for partying, girlfriends, boyfriends, even love.

Looking after your body will help you stay healthy, and understanding your emotions will help you explain to other people how you feel.

It is important to remember that everybody develops at their own rate and there are no rights and wrongs for how and when your body develops.

BODY SHAPES

As they grow, the differences between boys and girls become clearer. From an early age, boys tend to be thinner than girls but may be stronger and more muscular. As adults, men have broader shoulders and narrower hips than women. The female body becomes more rounded. Breasts grow on the wall of the chest and the hips become broader so there is room for a baby during pregnancy.

THE MALE AND FEMALE BODY

At birth, boys and girls look very similar. The only visible difference is that a boy has a penis and a scrotum containing two testicles, and a girl doesn't. Her sexual organs – ovaries, womb and vagina – are concealed inside her body, low down in her abdomen.

Men grow on average 7.5 cm taller than women. They tend to have longer arms and legs and bigger hands and feet. Their skull is larger and their bones bigger and denser.

MALE SEXUAL ORGANS

The penis is connected to both the bladder and the testicles. In childhood, it has only one role – to get rid of urine through a tube from the bladder, called the urethra. After puberty, the penis has a second role. During sex, it carries a fluid called semen containing millions of tadpole-shaped sperm cells, which are produced in the testicles.

Semen, which is made in special stores near the bladder, called seminal vesicles, also contains

As boys and girls develop into adults, their bodies develop differently. Many teenagers are very aware of this and find that they feel awkward with friends of the opposite sex.

nutrients for the sperm. These are made in the last of the male sexual organs, called the prostate. This gland is wrapped around the urethra where it leads out of the bladder.

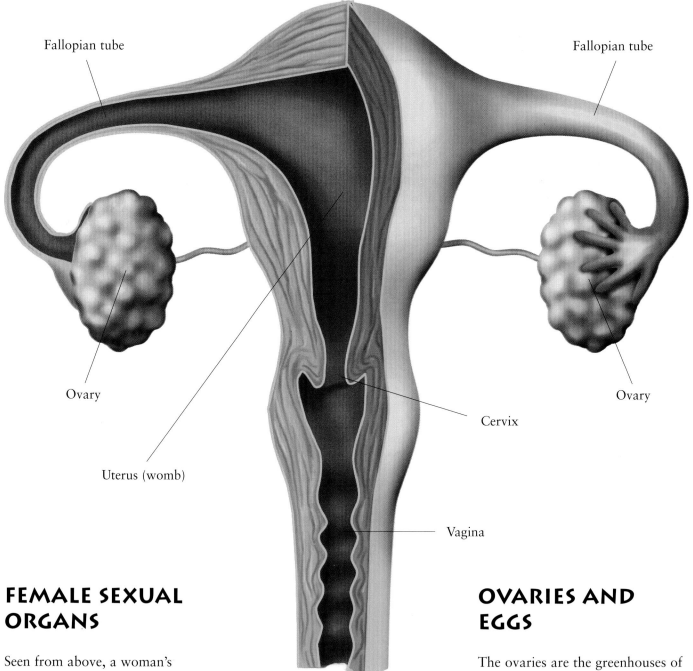

Fallopian tube

Fallopian tube

Ovary

Ovary

Uterus (womb)

Cervix

Vagina

FEMALE SEXUAL ORGANS

Seen from above, a woman's sexual organs look rather like the head of a goat. In the position of the face, is the womb, or uterus. This is a remarkably strong, muscular bag which is capable of stretching to 30 times its normal size to accommodate the growing foetus during pregnancy. On each side of the upper part of the womb – extending like a goat's horns – are the Fallopian tubes which link the ovaries to the womb.

The uterus changes dramatically during a woman's life. From puberty to menopause the lining of the uterus grows each month and gets ready to receive a fertilized egg. If the egg is not fertilized, the lining is shed during menstruation. During pregnancy, the uterus expands to allow the foetus to grow. It also protects and feeds the foetus. Before puberty and after menopause the uterus has no function.

OVARIES AND EGGS

The ovaries are the greenhouses of the female body. When a girl is born, her ovaries contain all the eggs that she will release during the years when she is fertile – and hundreds more that will be rejected. Each egg that is released is wafted down the Fallopian tube towards the uterus. If it meets some sperm along the way it may be fertilized, start to grow into an embryo and become attached to the wall of the uterus.

If it is not fertilized it will pass straight through the uterus, down into the vagina, through a narrow opening called the cervix.

The vagina is a hollow tube which leads from the cervical canal to the outside of the body. Like the womb, it can stretch – a small amount to make room for a man's penis during sex, and a much larger amount to let a baby out during childbirth.

THE VULVA

The vaginal opening lies just behind the urethra, the tube from the bladder through which urine is released. This area is called the vulva. Around the vaginal opening are protective, lip-shaped folds of skin called the labia. Hidden under these folds, at the front of the vaginal opening, is the clitoris. This is like a tiny penis and, like the penis, it swells during sex.

This picture has been artificially coloured. It shows an egg being released into the Fallopian tube during ovulation.

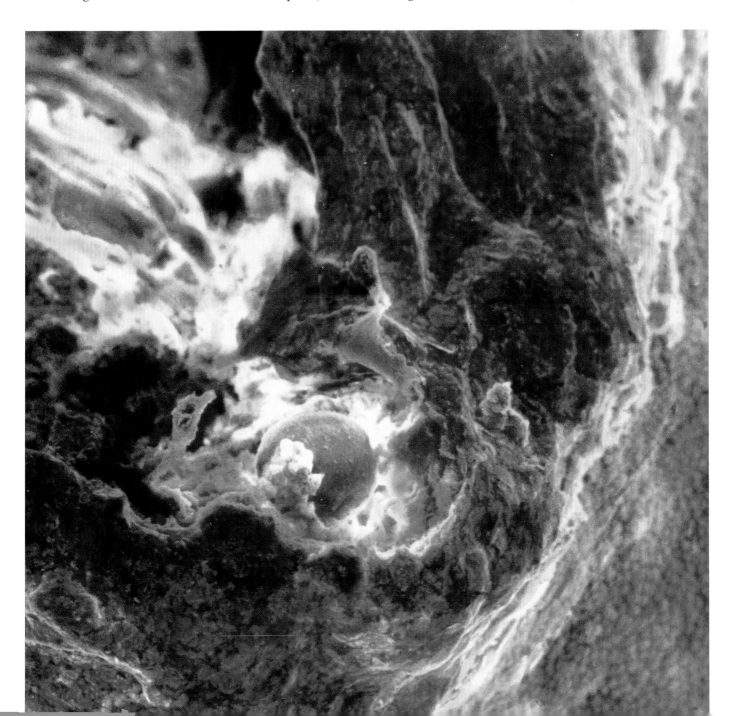

GIRLS AT PUBERTY

Girls officially reach puberty when their periods start. There's no set age for that to happen but it does seem to be happening slightly earlier than it used to. It also depends a little on the age that a girl's mother started her periods. If your mum was early, you'll probably be early, if she was late, you may have to wait too.

THE FEMALE BODY

Before her periods start, oestrogen makes a girl's nipples and then her breasts grow and her body becomes more rounded. It also makes hair grow under her arms and around her genitals. When she is about 13, a girl's oestrogen levels begin to rise and fall in a roughly 28-day cycle. Other hormones are also needed for her ovaries to produce eggs and her uterus to prepare for the possible arrival of an embryo.

As a girl develops into a young woman she becomes more aware of her body and her sexuality.

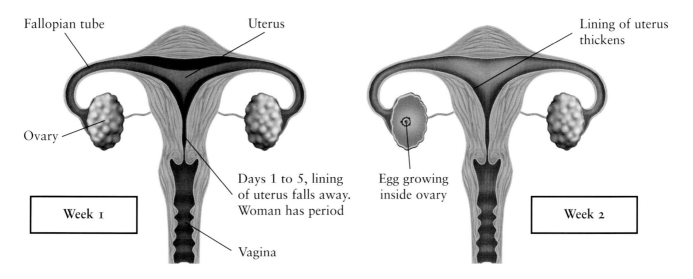

Week 1

Fallopian tube

Uterus

Ovary

Days 1 to 5, lining of uterus falls away. Woman has period

Vagina

Lining of uterus thickens

Egg growing inside ovary

Week 2

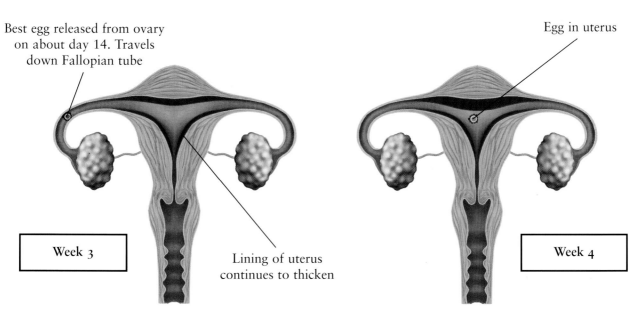

Best egg released from ovary on about day 14. Travels down Fallopian tube

Week 3

Lining of uterus continues to thicken

Egg in uterus

Week 4

THE MENSTRUAL CYCLE

The control centre for these hormones is not in the ovaries but in the brain, in neighbouring parts, called the hypothalamus and the pituitary gland. On day 1 of the menstrual cycle, when a woman starts her period, her body is already getting ready to produce and release an egg from one of her ovaries.

The hypothalamus produces luteinising hormone releasing hormone – LHRH for short.

This makes the pituitary gland release two hormones – follicle stimulating hormone (FSH) and luteinising hormone (LH) into the bloodstream.

During the menstrual cycle the hormone oestrogen is produced. This stimulates the growth of the lining of the womb as well as producing a secretion that makes it easier for the sperm to swim into the womb.

HORMONES

Puberty doesn't happen overnight. At the age of about 11, a girl's ovaries start to produce a hormone called oestrogen. This is the primary female reproductive hormone; it triggers most of the changes in the shape of a girl's body during adolescence and it plays an extremely important part in the menstrual cycle.

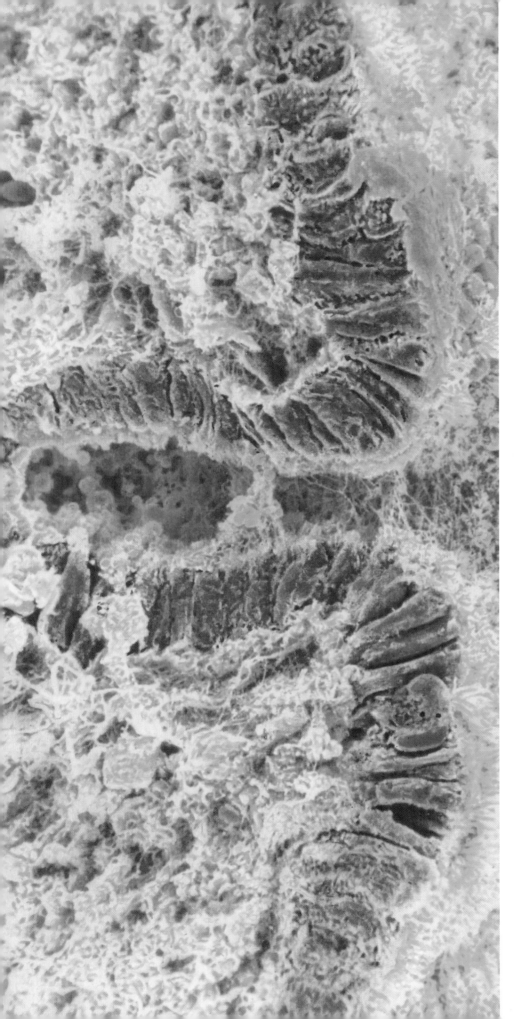

WHAT IS A PERIOD?

When FSH arrives at the ovary it makes several eggs start to grow, and when LH gets there it stimulates oestrogen production. By the end of a woman's period, on about day 5 of the menstrual cycle, the lining of the uterus starts to thicken, ready to receive an embryo.

Rising levels of oestrogen not only prepare the womb for a possible pregnancy they also have a feedback effect on FSH and LH so that both these hormones peak around day 14 of the cycle. At this point the best egg is released from the ovary – a process called ovulation.

WHAT HAPPENS DURING A PERIOD?

Its empty container, or follicle, begins to release a hormone called progesterone and small amounts of oestrogen. Together these two hormones keep the lining of the uterus in good shape until the egg has passed through during the second half of the menstrual cycle. At around day 28, all hormone levels drop. Since there is no embryo, the lining of the uterus falls away and the woman has her period. This is when a woman bleeds from her vagina. There isn't a lot of blood – about half a teacup comes out over four or five days.

This artificially coloured picture shows a section through the uterus. This is at day 22 in the menstrual cycle, when the lining of the uterus is building up to nourish an embryo.

THE RISK OF PREGNANCY

However, any young woman who has reached puberty should assume that she does ovulate and could, therefore, become pregnant if she has sex without contraception. For pregnancy to occur, the female egg must be fertilized by sperm within a few days of leaving the ovary. But, without monthly hormone tests, it is impossible to be sure when ovulation occurs. Some women ovulate earlier than usual in their monthly cycle, others later. It is therefore very risky to have sex without contraception at any time during the month, unless you want to become pregnant.

DID YOU KNOW?

★ Few women have a precise 28-day menstrual cycle, particularly when they first have periods. During adolescence, periods may be irregular. In some cycles an egg will be released, in others it won't.

Periods affect different women in different ways. Some women feel tired and run down, others find that they are hardly affected at all. Every woman is different.

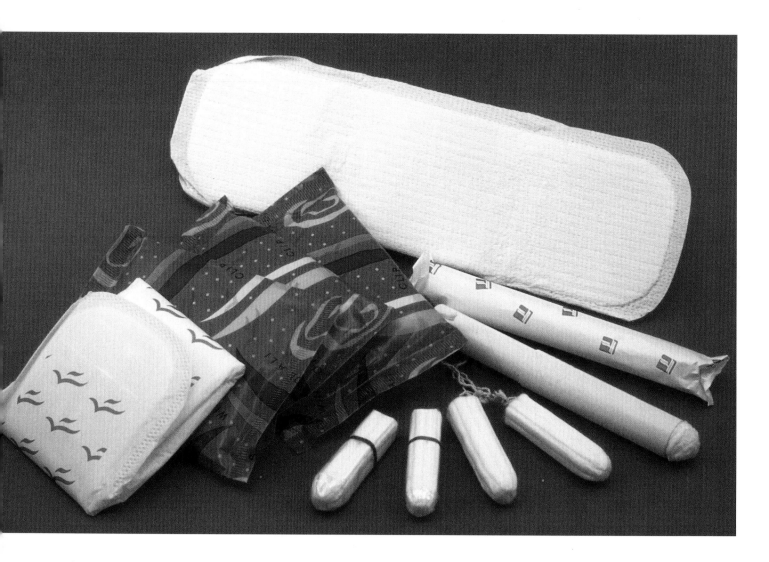

SANITARY PROTECTION

As they get near to the age of puberty, girls also need to look at the pads and tampons they will use when they get their period. There are lots of brands and it's worth trying several to find out which you like best. Some women use pads which fit into their underpants, while others use tampons which they insert into their vagina. Both pads and tampons are very effective. They need to be changed regularly during a period, and some women need to change them more often than others. Some lose more blood in the first day or two of their period, others on the second or third day.

TAMPONS

Using tampons can occasionally cause infection. This is why women should not use a more absorbent brand than they need and they should change their tampon as often as recommended on the packet, usually every four to eight hours. Toxic Shock Syndrome is a very serious illness caused by leaving tampons inside the body for more than the recommended time (normally about 6 hours).

Above Sanitary protection comes in many different forms. This selection of sanitary towels and tampons shows the range of products available. The only way to find out what is best for you is to try out the different options.

Right Most people wear a deodorant to reduce the amount of sweat which is released and make it smell nicer.

PERSONAL HYGIENE

Both girls and boys produce smellier sweat after puberty. Their new hormones produced at puberty switch on a new set of sweat glands, called the apocrine glands, under the arms, around the nipples and around the genitals. These produce much stronger sweat than the eccrine glands which cover the rest of the body. It contains chemicals which bacteria like to feed on, and it is these tiny microbes which make people smell. This is why people need to wash more often and more carefully after puberty. They need to get rid of all the smelly sweat.

BOYS AT PUBERTY

group of testicular cells, called Leydig cells, produce the male hormone, testosterone. Testosterone is also needed to make sperm grow, and for all the other changes to the male body which occur at puberty. The penis and testicles get larger, muscles develop and the chest becomes broader. The voice box (larynx) also gets bigger and the voice deeper. Hair grows more thickly on many parts of the body, first under the arms and at the base of the penis and, later, on the face. Some men gradually develop a hairy chest and stomach and may have hair on their shoulders and back too.

WHAT IS AN ERECTION?

Testosterone is also needed for erections. Inside the penis, a mass of spongy tissue surrounds the urethra. During an erection, nerve stimulation and testosterone make blood vessels in the penis fill up with blood. This makes the penis bigger and stiffer so that it becomes erect.

Even before puberty, boys sometimes have small erections.

BODY CHANGES

Like girls, male puberty happens quite slowly. Curiously, the growth and development of the testicles is controlled by FSH and LH – the same hormones that are important

The main stages in male physical development are the changes in body shape and the growth of pubic hair.

in the menstrual cycle. FSH from the pituitary gland stimulates the development of sperm cells in the testicles and LH makes another

WHAT IS A WET DREAM?

Erections also occur while men are asleep, and they may ejaculate. This is called a wet dream. Semen is released from the tip of the penis, causing a wet patch on pyjamas or bedding. Some men remember having a nice dream, others nothing at all.

After puberty these become larger and more frequent. At first, they may happen without warning when they aren't wanted. This is because your body takes time to adapt to all the extra hormones that are rushing about, and your penis may be super-sensitive for a while. When men start releasing semen during ejaculation, they are almost certainly releasing sperm cells too. This means that, if they have sex with a woman, they could make her pregnant. This is why it is so important to be sure to use contraception as soon as you start having sex, unless you want your partner to have a baby.

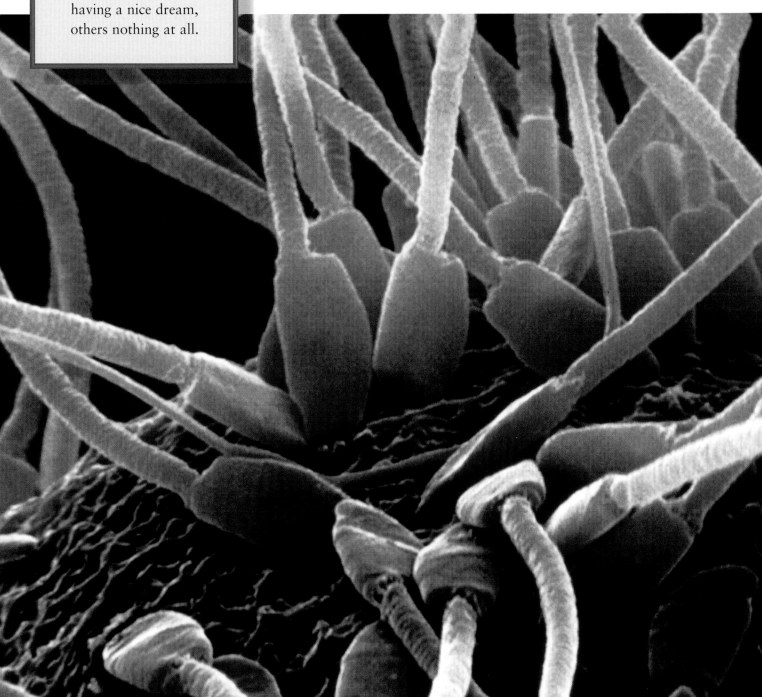

These sperm are clustered on the surface of a human egg (ovum). Each sperm has a head and a tail. The head is used to attach the sperm to the egg and to penetrate it and fertilize the egg nucleus.

BODY SHAPES

Just as young women change shape at different rates, so young men go through the bodily changes of puberty at different times. While girls wonder why their breasts haven't developed or their periods haven't started, boys worry that their voice hasn't broken or because they feel they look weedy. Unfortunately, you can't hurry puberty. It goes at its own pace. But it does happen in the end.

FACIAL HAIR

At puberty, adolescent men start to grow fine hair on their upper lip and chin. This slowly becomes thicker and stronger, but it is some time before it spreads up the sides of the face. Some young men decide to start shaving as soon as the hair is noticeable, others wait until it is thicker. It's some time before they need to shave every day.

Boys are under just as much pressure to conform and 'grow up' as girls. If a boy's body isn't developing as quickly as his friends' bodies he may be teased for being 'weedy'.

DEODORANTS

Like girls, boys are smellier after puberty if they do not wash carefully and use a deodorant. They too release stronger sweat. Two things in a deodorant will help you smell better. One is an anti-perspirant and the other is a mild perfume. Most anti-perspirants contain a zinc salt which dissolve in the sweat to form plugs. These block the pores and reduce the amount of sweat that is released. The perfumes which are added are very mild. Some are designed specially for men while others are unisex and just give you a fresh smell.

SHAVING PRODUCTS

There are lots of different types of razor to choose from; some are battery or electrically operated. It's a good idea to go to a pharmacy or supermarket to look at different types of razor and to ask friends and family which brands they like. If you shave in the same direction that the hair grows, you are less likely to irritate your skin.

Advertising campaigns for new shaving products are constantly on the television. Rather than trying every new product on the market, try and get advice from men you know who shave.

GROWTH

Adolescence is a very important growing time. By the end of adolescence, young men and women are as tall as they will ever be. Their final height will depend on the genes they inherited from their parents, how much growth hormone they produced, and the amount and types of food they ate.

GROWTH HORMONE

Growth hormone makes people grow by working on special cells at one end of bones. As the bones all over the body get longer, people get taller. If this happened throughout life, we would all become giants. But, at the end of adolescence, the bone cells stop responding to growth hormone and growth stops.

Your parents are a good indication of the kind of height you may reach, but even then you may find that you suddenly have a growth spurt or stop growing earlier than your parents did.

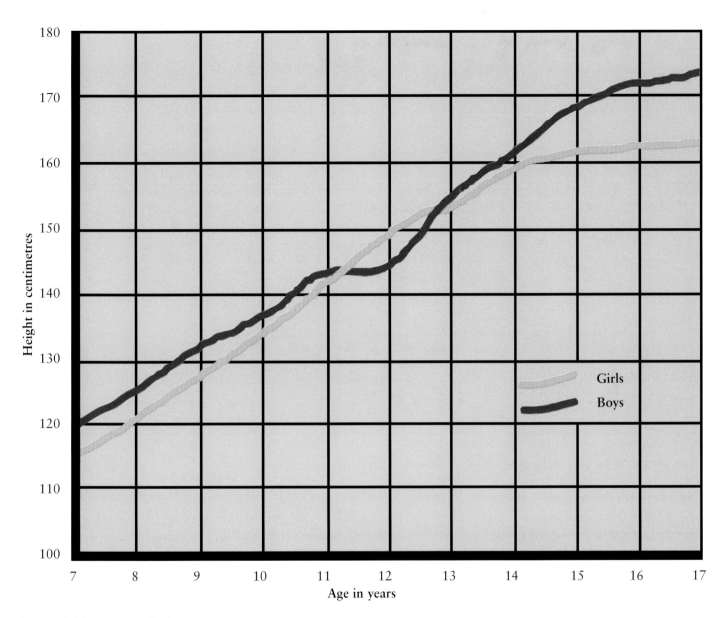

Boys and girls grow at a similar rate until around 13 when girls' heights stabilize and boys continue to grow.

CHANGES INSIDE YOUR BODY

Growth hormone not only makes people grow in height, it also boosts the growth of muscles and organs such as the heart and lungs, and it changes the way the body handles sugar and fat, so there is more energy available to fuel all the extra growth.

TRUE OR FALSE?

Most people grow roughly as tall as their parents.
True. Tall people tend to have tall children and short people often have short children. Children with one tall and one short parent may be tall, short or medium sized. Growth is controlled by a hormone called somatotrophin, also known as growth hormone. It is made in the pituitary gland. But, like the sex hormones, release of growth hormone is controlled by two further hormones, called somatostatin and growth hormone releasing factor (GH-RF), produced in the hypothalamus. GH-RF stimulates the release of growth hormone while somatostatin blocks it.

NUTRITION FOR THE FUTURE

Good nutrition is also essential for growth. The body needs a mixture of protein, fat, carbohydrate, minerals and vitamins so that it can grow and develop normally. If anything is missing, growth problems can occur.

GROWTH SPURTS

Throughout childhood, boys and girls grow steadily, with occasional short spurts. Most grow an average 5 cm per year. But, as they approach puberty, their growth patterns change. At the same time that a girl's oestrogen levels rise, she also starts a major growth spurt, growing up to 9 cm in a year. This lasts two to four years.

Boys begin their growth spurt later, so for a while they may be shorter than girls of the same age. The adolescent male growth spurt usually starts at 12 or 13. Young men also grow about 5 cm per year. But their growth spurt goes on a year or so longer than women, so they end up an average 7.5 cm taller.

WHEN WILL YOU GROW?

Children who are late reaching puberty may worry that they are not growing as fast as some of their friends. They just need to be patient. If they grew at a normal rate during childhood, they have plenty of growth hormone and don't need injections. When puberty comes, they will grow too.

Above The saying 'you are what you eat' is very apt. If you start life eating healthily you are giving your body the fuel it needs to work well – you are giving yourself a head start.

Right This 11-year-old boy is being treated with injections of a growth hormone because his body does not produce enough. His doctor is measuring his height in order to check how well the treatment is working.

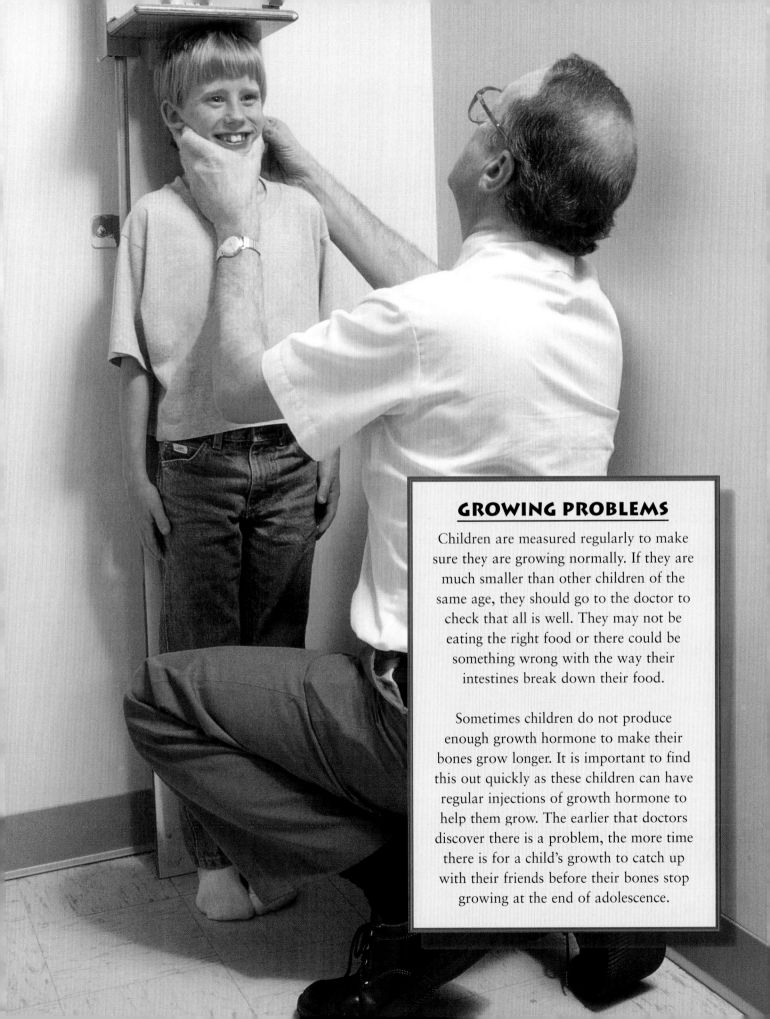

GROWING PROBLEMS

Children are measured regularly to make sure they are growing normally. If they are much smaller than other children of the same age, they should go to the doctor to check that all is well. They may not be eating the right food or there could be something wrong with the way their intestines break down their food.

Sometimes children do not produce enough growth hormone to make their bones grow longer. It is important to find this out quickly as these children can have regular injections of growth hormone to help them grow. The earlier that doctors discover there is a problem, the more time there is for a child's growth to catch up with their friends before their bones stop growing at the end of adolescence.

SKIN PROBLEMS

Very few young people – male or female – get through adolescence without the odd batch of spots. It's called acne. Some are plagued by armies of painful, red, inflamed pimples that become filled with pus and never seem to go away. But there's no need to suffer in silence. In fact, it's important to get effective treatment to prevent scarring of the skin.

ACNE

Acne occurs because the skin over-reacts to testosterone. At puberty, boys have a big increase in testosterone production, and girls make a little of it too.

The skin is a very versatile organ. It is tough enough to project and shield our other organs; it is waterproof and it protects us from sunlight. It can keep heat in or help us to cool off.

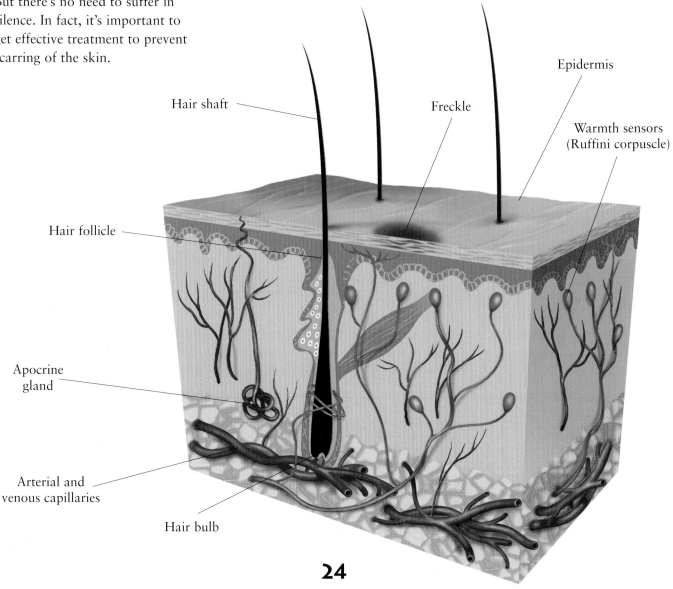

Hair shaft

Freckle

Epidermis

Warmth sensors
(Ruffini corpuscle)

Hair follicle

Apocrine
gland

Arterial and
venous capillaries

Hair bulb

WHAT CAUSES SPOTS?

In the skin, testosterone activates the sebaceous glands so that they start producing a greasy substance, called sebum, to lubricate the skin. The glands are attached to thin tubes, called follicles, which contain the fine hairs on the skin, so grease trickles on to the surface. Adolescent men and women who get spots produce normal amounts of testosterone but their sebaceous glands release too much grease. This makes the cells which line their hair follicles very sticky, and they gradually clog up the tubes. The grease cannot escape and solidifies in the follicle. These plugs become discoloured and form blackheads and whiteheads on the surface of the skin.

Many young people are already very self-conscious, so getting acne can often seem like the end of the world.

WHAT MAKES A SPOT?

If harmless bacteria which live on everyone's skin break down the greasy plugs in the hair follicles, chemicals are released which irritate the skin. It becomes inflamed and spots form which may become filled with pus and form a yellowish pustule. In the end, this bursts, the pus is released and the spot starts to heal. Some spots get very big before they burst or calm down and these can leave scars.

HOW CAN YOU TREAT ACNE?

Like any health problem, acne needs treatment. You can buy products from the pharmacy and, if these don't work, your doctor can prescribe stronger medicines. One popular product you can buy is called benzoyl peroxide. It cuts down the amount of grease produced by the sebaceous glands, loosens blackheads and reduces the number of bacteria. You should see some improvement in your acne within six to eight weeks.

At first, benzoyl peroxide may irritate the skin, but usually improves with time. However, if your skin gets very sore you should stop using it and see your pharmacist or doctor.

MEDICAL ADVICE

If benzoyl peroxide does not help your spots, your doctor can prescribe antibiotics to get rid of the bacteria which cause the infected pustules. Antibiotics can be used as creams or, in more difficult cases, taken as tablets. Courses last several weeks or months. If they do not work, there are other drugs to try. Women can use one specific brand of oral contraceptive pill which reduces grease production in the skin. This treatment takes at least 12 months to clear up the acne.

HELP YOURSELF

Acne is no one's fault. It doesn't mean you are dirty or eat the wrong things. You are just more sensitive to testosterone than other people. Everyone should wash every day, whether they have acne or not. But washing several times a day to try and get rid of spots isn't a good idea. It will just make the skin dry and sore. Some people find it helpful to wash with anti-bacterial solutions they can buy at the pharmacy or supermarket.

Although acne is not usually due to an unhealthy diet, a good diet will keep the general health of your skin good.

HEALTHY SKIN: HEALTHY DIET

Eating plenty of fresh fruit and vegetables is good for the whole body, not just the skin. Fatty food, lack of exercise, smoking and alcohol do not cause acne, but they can make the skin look tired and grey. If your spots are making you miserable, you can buy creams to cover them up.

The pharmacist can help you choose a good brand, but look for those that are labelled 'non-greasy.' If you're staying in, give your skin a rest and always be sure to get all the cover-up cream off your face at the end of the day.

Right It is best to seek advice from your doctor or pharmacist when looking for new treatments for skin conditions.

ISOTRETINOIN

Another acne treatment, called isotretinoin, works in several ways to reduce the amount of grease in the skin, unblock follicles and prevent infection. It can be used by both men and women but does have several unwanted effects. For example, people get chapped lips and dry, itchy skin. It's best to see a skin specialist who can discuss these problems. Treatment usually lasts four to six months.

EMOTIONS

ROLLERCOASTER EMOTIONS

The changes which happen to the body during adolescence are not just physical. They affect feelings and emotions too. Those new hormones don't just make breasts and penises bigger, and give you spots, they affect your mind as well. They can make you happy, sad, angry, anxious, depressed, elated; and that's just on Monday! Sometimes you may feel like you're on a rollercoaster of emotions – high as the sky one minute, down in the dumps the next. It doesn't help that you're probably surrounded by dozens of other adolescents all in the same boat, with their hormones all over the place too. Friends – and enemies – may start acting differently.

PLAYING GOOSEBERRY

When two young people get together as a couple, it affects their friends as well. Some may feel rejected, especially if they don't have a boyfriend or girlfriend. All children know how miserable they feel when their best friend goes off with someone else. Before puberty, it's usually another girl or another boy. During adolescence it may be someone of the opposite sex, but it can hurt just as much. Young

people who don't have boyfriends or girlfriends can feel very left out, especially if puberty is affecting them more slowly and they still look more like children than adults. It's easy to start thinking there's something wrong – physically or emotionally – especially if family or class-mates make fun of you. You get anxious or depressed and that just makes things worse.

Above It is very hard for a couple who are very involved with each other to avoid their friends feeling left out.

Right During adolescence friendships can be very tempestuous. One minute you are the best of friends, the next you are fighting all the time.

BOY OR GIRLFRIENDS?

Until puberty, children tend to be most friendly with those of their own sex. Many girls think boys are stupid and lots of boys think the same about girls. During adolescence, this changes. Young men and women mix more, some form strong attachments and start going around as a couple. It's not just physical attraction. They may like the same bands, think about things in the same way, or just enjoy hanging around together.

SHARE YOUR FEELINGS

Talking to people about your problems often helps. You'll soon realize that others are going through the same thing. Even those who are going out with the most gorgeous girl or boy in class won't have everything their way. Relationships are never easy, especially when you're new to them. Girlfriends and boyfriends can upset you, go off you, start going out with someone else. It's not as easy as it looks!

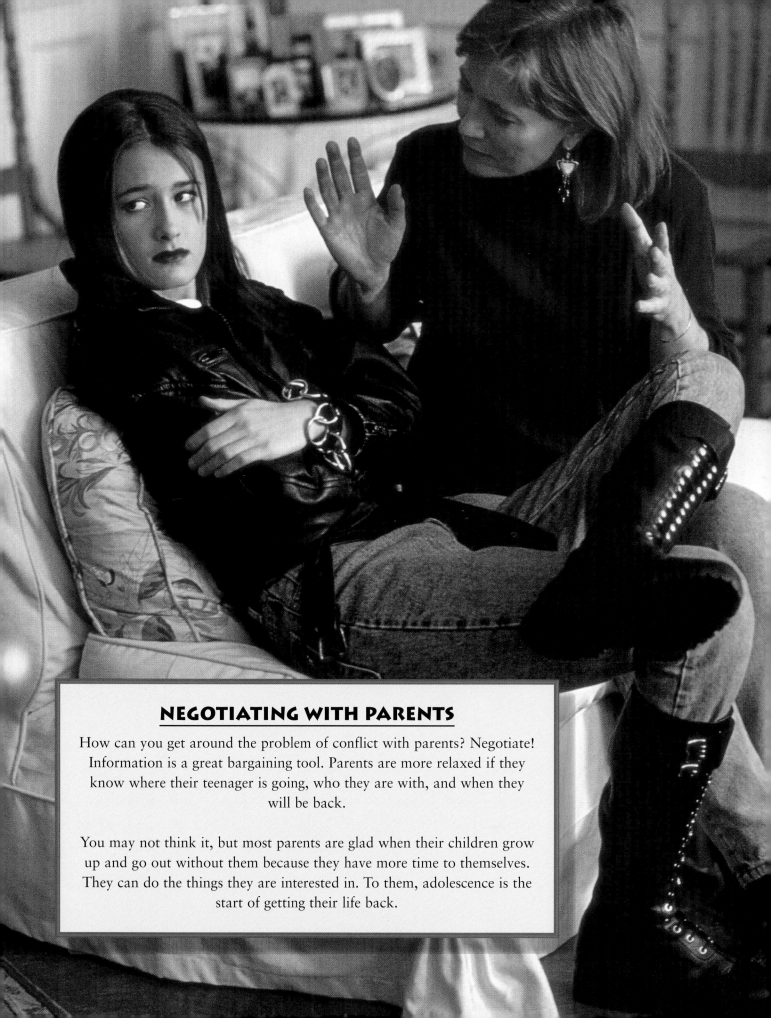

NEGOTIATING WITH PARENTS

How can you get around the problem of conflict with parents? Negotiate!
Information is a great bargaining tool. Parents are more relaxed if they
know where their teenager is going, who they are with, and when they
will be back.

You may not think it, but most parents are glad when their children grow
up and go out without them because they have more time to themselves.
They can do the things they are interested in. To them, adolescence is the
start of getting their life back.

Left Adolescence doesn't have to be a time of constant conflict with your parents. Like any relationship, if you talk to your parents, discussions will be easier.

Below Many teenagers find that they feel frustrated by their family's reluctance to let them become their own person. Hard as it may be, a little tolerance from both sides makes negotiation easier.

TROUBLE AT HOME

During adolescence, young men and women who are starting to look like adults want to act like them too. They want to make their own decisions and choose how they spend their time and who they spend it with. As they get older, they don't want adults, such as parents and teachers, to tell them what to do. They want to be independent.

This change isn't easy for anyone. Parents worry that if they are not around to help, young people will get into trouble. Adolescents call it interfering and making a fuss.

KEEPING PARENTS INFORMED

If you tell them your plans, show that you have thought things through, they'll be able to do their thing without worrying about where you are. Slowly, your lives will separate until you're ready to leave home and get your own place.

This gradual move towards independence is sure to have its bad patches. No one gets through adolescence without being nagged about their loud music, their untidy room, their sub-standard school reports and their undesirable friends. Who wants to be a caring, responsible citizen at 15?

Left Unhappiness in adolescence can be related to mood swings and pass fairly quickly or it can be a longer term depression that needs treatment.

DEALING WITH UNHAPPINESS

More young people are depressed than ever before. Life today seems to make some of them anxious and unhappy in a way that earlier generations escaped. They express their unhappiness in different ways. They may be moody and irritable, easily upset and tearful, or get a lot of minor ailments, such as head and stomach aches. They can't concentrate and may have trouble sleeping. They spend a lot of time on their own. Life may seem pointless.

EATING DISORDERS

More and more young people use food to try and deal with their negative feelings about themselves and their lives. Some starve themselves until they are dangerously thin but won't accept that there is anything wrong. This is called anorexia nervosa. Others binge on huge amounts of food and then make themselves sick so that they won't put on weight. This is bulimia nervosa.

A third group are compulsive eaters. They also eat large amounts of food but, as they do not vomit afterwards, they tend to put on weight. They then try to diet. They yo-yo backwards and forwards between eating too much and too little, without ever establishing a healthy eating pattern.

DANGERS OF EATING DISORDERS

All three of these eating disorders are bad for the body; anorexia can kill or permanently damage the heart, kidneys or other organs, make the bones brittle and prone to fracture, and lead to infertility in later life.

SEEKING HELP

Whatever the reason for the eating disorder, it is vital to get help before permanent damage is done. Severe anorexia may need treatment in hospital. But anyone with an eating disorder needs help to find out what is wrong and how to deal with it without starving or overeating. This may mean all the family talking with a specially trained therapist to find out what is going wrong.

Media images of very thin models add to the pressure to look good during adolescence. This means that some young people become obsessed with dieting.

DID YOU KNOW?

★ Eating disorders – particularly anorexia and bulimia – are more common in young women than in young men. This may be partly due to the pressures on adolescent women to look and dress like the rich and famous models, actresses and singers they see on TV and in magazines.

★ Some young women may use anorexia to delay puberty and put off growing up. Being very underweight stops breast development and the start of periods. Others simply use eating as their way of dealing with great unhappiness in their life, at home or at school.

HELPING OTHERS

If you or someone you know has a problem with alcohol, smoking or illegal drugs, you can get help. Some organizations are listed at the end of this book. They won't judge you, they'll just try to help.

DRINK AND DRUGS

Adolescence is a time when people experiment. They change school, make new friends, start going places without their family. They try things out; some of the things they try are really bad for them. Eight out of 10 children have had their first taste of alcohol by the time they are 10. By the age of 15, a third of young women and over a quarter of young men smoke regularly. Nearly half of young people have tried illegal drugs by the time they are 16.

BECOMING ADDICTED

When you start using alcohol, cigarettes and illegal drugs, it's hard to stop. Each year, over 1,000 young people under 15 in the UK need emergency treatment for alcohol poisoning. Two 13-year-olds recently became the youngest people to die in the UK from heroin overdoses and, since 1987, about 70 deaths have been linked to ecstasy. Most of the victims were young people.

Left Whatever problems or worries you have during adolescence, it is never healthy to bottle them up. Talking to friends or family may not provide magic solutions, but it may help you to put the problem into perspective.

SMOKING KILLS

Cigarettes kill more slowly. It usually takes at least 10 years of regular smoking to get lung cancer, sometimes longer. But lungs can get inflamed, swollen and painful with just a few years of smoking. Most smokers have an early morning cough; their lungs release mucus and fluid to try and protect them from the toxic effects of the

Ask most smokers if they regret having started smoking and they'll tell you 'yes'. It's worth thinking hard before you take up smoking.

poisons in tobacco smoke, and these build up in the night when smokers lie still. In the morning they need to cough them up and spit them out.

SEX

This chapter won't tell you how to have sex. When you feel ready, it will help you give and get enjoyment from your body, and your partner's, and it will explain how to look after your sexual health.

SENSITIVITY

With large dollops of sex hormones in their bloodstream after puberty, most young people take a new interest in their own and other people's bodies.

NERVE ENDINGS

In the skin are thousands of nerve endings. Nerves carry messages from one part of the body to another. In the skin, they detect outside stimuli – heat and cold, pain and pleasure – and send messages to the brain about them. The most sensitive parts of the human body, such as the skin on the genitals, breasts and face, have most nerve endings. The hormones released during puberty make these nerve endings especially responsive; it's a bit like switching on the Christmas tree lights!

Your body belongs to you and you should never feel pressurized into doing anything that you feel unhappy about or uncomfortable with.

Large areas of the skin, which they never thought about before, suddenly seem to be much more sensitive when they touch them.

For most couples, developing a good friendship and getting to know one another is an essential first-step to forming a relationship.

Not just the penis and vulva, but breasts and nipples, the insides of the thighs, shoulders and lower backs, faces.

Touching and stroking the most sensitive parts of the body gives a lot of pleasure. Everyone varies a little, and it takes time to find out what feels nicest. If you're uncomfortable and tense, nothing feels very good! So it's best to be warm, comfortable and relaxed.

RELAXING TOGETHER

Some people need more touching than others, and sometimes their skin is more sensitive than other times. If they are nervous or scared, they won't get much pleasure from touching and stroking, even if it goes on for a long time. They'll be thinking about what is worrying them and won't be able to relax.

Masturbation is one way adolescents have found out for themselves what makes their body feel good.

PLEASING YOURSELF

When they touch or stroke their own body, most people can relax and enjoy themselves. It may not happen straight away, especially if they are worried about what they are doing. At some time, we've all heard or read that touching or stroking our body, especially our 'privates' is wrong. Years ago, boys were warned they'd go blind if they played with their penis, or it would drop off!

Before two people start to touch and stroke each other, they need to feel relaxed together. That's easier if they are good friends and care about each other, know each others likes and dislikes. It takes time to get to know and trust someone, especially to become physically close. It's called being intimate. If one partner feels they are being rushed, they may back off and the friendship will fade.

TRUE OR FALSE?

Masturbation is harmful.
False. Masturbating – touching, stroking and rubbing your penis or clitoris – does not damage your health. If you rub too hard, you may make yourself sore, and it's antisocial to do it in public. But it isn't wrong or bad.

THERE ARE NO RULES

There's no set timetable for sex, and it's worth taking the time to get to know each other's bodies first. Most couples start by kissing and cuddling, and may take weeks or months before they go further. Even when they start having sex, they spend some nights kissing, cuddling and massaging each other rather than having sex every time they are intimate.

Some couples choose not to have sex until they marry (chastity).

YOUR CHOICE

Sex is not compulsory with a boyfriend or girlfriend. If and when it does happen, both partners must want it. If you care enough about someone to want to have sex with them, also care enough about them to wait until they are ready. Urging someone to have sex when they do not want to is sure to end in failure.

LEARNING THE ROPES

Most people have found that sex is most enjoyable when it is part of a close, caring friendship. Some boast about having sex with people they've only just met, but few enjoy it very much. Sex, like most activities, takes practice. Couples need to learn what each likes doing when they have sex, and that's unlikely to happen the first time. They need to tell and show their partners what they enjoy. Some people like one thing, some another, and it's important to respect each other's likes and dislikes. If one partner isn't happy about taking part in a particular type of sex, it is wrong to bully or force them to do it.

YOUR SEXUAL HEALTH

Taking time to get to know someone before having sex also gives you a chance to talk about your sexual health. What type of contraception will you use?

It is always awkward discussing the contraception you and your partner will use. Once you've tackled the subject you'll both feel more relaxed.

CONTRACEPTION CHOICES

There are many different ways of preventing you or your partner from getting pregnant. Being careful – withdrawing the penis from the vagina before ejaculation – is not one of them. Even before a man comes, there may be a trickle of semen from his penis, with more than enough sperm to get his partner pregnant.

THE PILL

The most effective method of contraception is the contraceptive pill. This contains hormones which prevent ovulation, make it difficult for sperm to get near the female egg and/or change the lining of the uterus so that it isn't ready for an embryo.

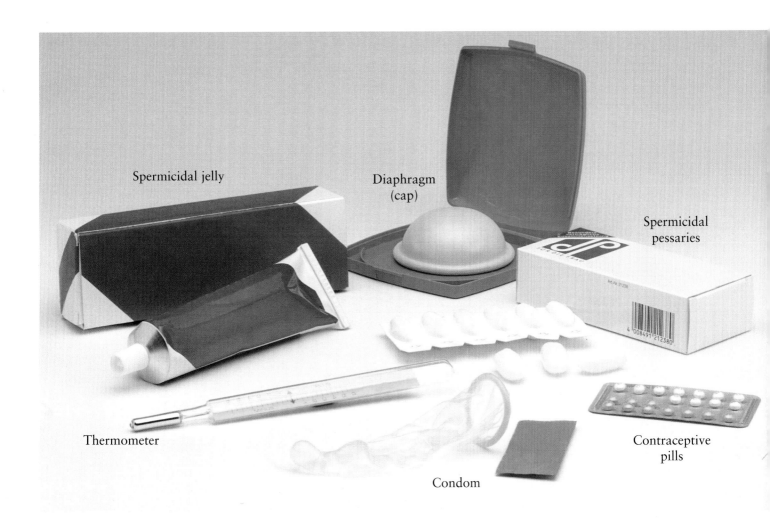

Spermicidal jelly

Diaphragm
(cap)

Spermicidal
pessaries

Thermometer

Condom

Contraceptive
pills

Thermometers are used in the 'rhythm method' to gauge when a woman is ovulating.

WHERE CAN YOU GET CONTRACEPTIVES?

You can buy condoms in pharmacies and lots of shops but women need a prescription from their doctor for the contraceptive pill. Like other drugs, the pill has unwanted effects and it is important to find out about all of these before starting treatment. For example, any woman who gets headaches or leg pain when taking the pill should tell her doctor straight away.

Trying to avoid having sex around the time a woman ovulates is another unreliable method of contraception. It is impossible to be sure when the egg is released without taking expensive hormone tests for several days around the middle of the menstrual cycle.

CONDOMS

Condoms can be nearly as effective as the pill in preventing pregnancy, and they also prevent infection from being passed from one partner to the other. This is more important now than ever before. There are so many infections which can be passed on during sex that it is important to use a condom even if you are using the pill to prevent pregnancy. Then you can be sure of not getting pregnant or catching or passing on an infection.

BEING SAFE

Both the pill and condoms have to be used correctly for them to work properly. The pill must be taken every day, usually for three out of every four weeks of the menstrual cycle. Condoms need to be worn every time you have sex. They are fiddly to use at first, so it's worth looking at a few, seeing how they unroll and trying them out on your own before using them for sex.

TEENAGE MOTHERS

Most teenagers know someone who became pregnant before they left school. These young women have to make a tough choice. They can end their pregnancy with an abortion. They can have their baby and give it to another family to bring up (adopt). Or they can bring it up themselves, usually with help from their own mum and family.

MISSING OUT ON THE FUN

Whatever they do, their life will never be the same again. If they have an abortion or have their child adopted they will always wonder what their child might be like. Many teenagers who decide to keep their baby do not finish school, so they find it hard to get a job later on. They also miss out on the fun of being young and care-free. If you use contraception when you have sex you can have a child when you are ready.

Above Many people find it embarrassing to use a condom, but if you are with a partner you care for and trust, you can share the experience and even laugh about it!

Right The pressure on very young parents is high. They may end up resenting each other – or their child – for 'taking away their freedom'.

WHO TO TURN TO

If you or someone you know thinks they are pregnant, they can get help. At the end of this book, there is a list of organizations to go to. The people who work there will not tell you off, but they will try to help.

PRESSURE TO SUCCEED

Today, there is more pressure on young people to do well than ever before. From an early age, they are told to get smart, get rich, get ahead. People judge us all on how we look, how we live, how we perform.

Everyone gets really 'down' during adolescence. It can be a tough time.

JUST BE YOURSELF

But everyone is different. We don't all look like supermodels or think like Einstein. We all have different skills and abilities, different likes and dislikes. The trick is to build on the things we are good at and

to worry less about those we can't do. You won't simply be able to give up all your worst subjects at school, but try being more confident in the things you do well. People get better at doing this as they get older. But adolescence is an excellent time to start.

Preventing unwanted pregnancies and sexually transmitted diseases, such as AIDS, are just some of the concerns that teenagers today have.

LOOKING AFTER YOUR SEXUAL HEALTH

If you look after your sexual health, you will protect yourself from serious infections such as AIDS, and you'll prevent yourself or your partner from becoming pregnant when you aren't ready. Adolescence is a great time, so why not give it your best shot – now and for the future.

STAY HEALTHY

It's also a good time to take more care of your health. If you look after yourself when you are young, you'll stay fitter all your life. Being overweight is bad for your heart and other organs. You may get away with it now, but it'll catch up with you sooner than you think. If you eat less fat and sugar now, you will be healthier later on. Exercise will help you stay fit too.

GLOSSARY

Abdomen The cavity which lies between the diaphragm and the pelvis and contains all the digestive organs such as the kidneys, liver and pancreas.

AIDS (acquired immune deficiency syndrome) A disease resulting from HIV (human immune deficiency virus) that breaks down the defence system of the body.

Bacteria Micro-organisms which can cause infection or live peacefully in the body all the time.

Carbohydrate A type of food (eg. pasta, bread, potato) containing sugars or starches.

Cell The smallest part of a living thing (eg. cell of human).

Cervix The neck of the uterus, through which an egg passes during each menstrual cycle or a baby at birth.

Chastity Making a decision not to have sex for religious or other reasons.

Clitoris A very sensitive organ in the female genitals.

Depression A severe unhappiness often needing professional treatment.

Ecstasy An illegal drug used to keep people awake and full of energy, it has harmful unwanted effects (eg. serious lack of fluids which can lead to unconsciousness and occasionally death).

Ejaculation The release of semen from the penis.

Embryo The early stage in the development of a baby in the womb.

Emotion A feeling (eg. happiness, anger, sadness, guilt).

Erection The enlargement and movement of the penis from its usual downward position to a more upright position.

Fallopian tube Part of the female reproductive system where fertilization of the egg occurs. It links the ovary to the uterus.

Fertile To be able to have children.

Foetus The later stage of the development of a baby in the womb.

Follicle A cavity in the body such as the hair follicle.

Gland A part of the body which produces hormones or other fluids.

Heroin An illegal addictive drug which can cause brain and other organ damage.

Hormone A substance that is produced in one part of the body which can work nearby or in another part of the body.

Menopause The period of time when a woman stops menstruating after which she can no longer become pregnant.

Mucus A thick fluid produced in the body after contact with microbes or dangerous gases etc (eg. colds, flu, cigarette smoke).

Muscle The tissues in the body that are responsible for movement and are very powerful.

Nucleus The central or most important part of an item, such as a cell, around which others are grouped.

Oestrogen Several hormones that are secreted by the ovaries and placenta that stimulate changes in the female reproductive organs.

Organ A unit in the body, such as the kidney, brain or skin.

Ovary The female organ that produces the eggs.

Ovum A human egg, that if fertilized, develops into a foetus.

Protein A type of food found in meat, fish, beans and nuts that forms the basic building blocks of the body.

Rhythm method A method of contraception which is based on measuring the woman's temperature. When the temperature drops it indicates that ovulation has taken place. This method is known to be unreliable.

Secretion When something is released, such as when pus is released from a spot.

Semen The fluid carrying millions of sperm which is released from the penis during ejaculation.

Synthetic When something is manufactured or 'man-made'.

Uterus The organ, also known as the womb, which is intended to nurture and protect the foetus.

Vagina Part of the female genitals which leads to the uterus.

FURTHER INFORMATION

FURTHER READING

Talking Points: Family Violence by Ronda Armitage (Wayland Publishers, 1999)
Life Files: Drugs by Julian Cohen (Evans Brothers, 1998)
What Kids Really Want to Know About Sex by Phillip Hodson (Robson Books, 1993)
Girls are from Saturn, Boys are from Jupiter by Kathryn Lamb (Piccadilly, 1998)
Talking Points: Mental Illness by Vanora Leigh (Wayland, 1999)
Drugs by Adrian King (Wayland, 1997)
New Diary of a Teenage Health Freak by Aidan Macfarlane, Anne McPherson (Oxford Paperbacks, 1987)
The Really Useful Teenage Food Guide by Janette Marshall (Vermillion, 1996)
Drinking Alcohol by Steve Myers and Pete Sanders (Franklin Watts, 1996)
Let's Discuss: Sex and Sexuality by Steve Myers and Pete Sanders (Franklin Watts, 1996)
Let's Discuss: Love, Hate and Other Feelings by Steve Myers and Pete Sanders (Franklin Watts, 1996)
What Do You Know About: Aids? by Steve Myers and Pete Sanders (Franklin Watts, 1996)
Just Don't Make a Scene Mum by Rosie Rushdon (Piccadilly, 1995)

Let's Talk About Smoking by Elizabeth Weitzman and Rudolf Steiner (Powerkids Press, 1998)
Health and Fitness: How Does My Diet Affect Me? by Patsy Westcott (Wayland Publishers, 1999)
Young Citizen: Growing Up by Kate Brookes (Wayland Publishers, 1999)

FINDING OUT MORE

Helpful Organizations

Alcohol Concern,
Waterbridge House,
32-36 Loman Street,
London SE1 0EE
Tel: 0207 9287377
www.alcoholconcern.org.uk

Brook Advisory Centres
(throughout UK)
Details on contraception clinics:
0800 0185 023

ChildLine,
Freepost 1111,
London N1 0BR
Freephone: 0800 1111
Website: www.childline.org.uk

Depression Alliance,
35, Westminster Bridge Road,
London SE1 7JB
Tel: 0207 633 0557

Scotland: 0131 467 3050
Wales: 01222 611674
Website: www.gn.apc.org/da/

Eating Disorders Association,
1st Floor,
103, Prince of Wales Road,
Norwich NR1 1DW
Helpline 01603 765050 (Monday-Friday 4-6pm)
Website: www.gurney.org.uk/eda/adolescence/40

Health Education Authority,
Trevelyan House,
30 Great Peter Street,
London SW1P 2HW
Tel: 0207 4131888
www.hea.org.uk

INDEX